11/16/11

Drawing Is Fun!

DRAWING
PETS AND FARM ANIMALS

Gareth Stevens
Publishing

Please visit our Web site, www.garethstevens.com. For a free color catalog of all our high-quality books, call toll free 1-800-542-2595 or fax 1-877-542-2596.

Library of Congress Cataloging-in-Publication Data

Cook, Trevor, 1948-
Drawing pets and farm animals / Trevor Cook and Lisa Miles.
     p. cm. — (Drawing is fun!)
Includes index.
ISBN 978-1-4339-5071-1 (pbk.)
ISBN 978-1-4339-5072-8 (6-pack)
ISBN 978-1-4339-5026-1 (library binding)
1. Animals in art—Juvenile literature. 2. Livestock in art—
Juvenile literature. 3. Drawing—Technique—Juvenile literature. I.
Miles, Lisa. II. Title.
NC780.C66 2011
743.6—dc22

2010027760

First Edition

Published in 2011 by
Gareth Stevens Publishing
111 East 14th Street, Suite 349
New York, NY 10003

Copyright © 2011 Arcturus Publishing

Artwork: Q2A India
Text: Trevor Cook and Lisa Miles
Editors: Fiona Tulloch and Joe Harris
Cover design: Akihiro Nakayama

Picture credits: All photographs supplied by Shutterstock.

Printed in United States

CPSIA compliance information: Batch #AW11GS: For further information contact Gareth Stevens, New York, New York at 1-800-542-2595.

SL001767US

Contents

Dog

This dog has excellent hearing.

He has a wet nose. This helps him to follow smells.

His fur grows longer in winter.

He wags his tail when he's happy.

FUN FACTS ● FUN FACTS ● FUN FACTS ● FUN FACTS ● FUN FACTS

Puppies are born with their eyes closed. They open their eyes after around two weeks!

1. Start with a shape like a banana.

2. Now put on two legs and start on his head.

3. Now add his tail, the other legs, and the rest of his face.

4. Add his tongue. Make his nose look shiny.

Goldfish

This goldfish has seven fins.

He has shiny scales.

Goldfish can be red, brown, yellow, white, orange, or black.

His fins help him to swim through the water.

FUN FACTS ● FUN FACTS ● FUN FACTS ● FUN FACTS ● FUN FACTS

People have Kept goldfish as pets for around 1,000 years.

1. This is the shape of his body.

2. Put on his face.

3. Now add some more fins.

4. He's yellow and orange.

Hamster

She has pouches in her mouth. She carries food in them.

This hamster has two sharp front teeth.

She likes digging! She uses her claws to dig.

She has long whiskers.

FUN FACTS ● FUN FACTS ● FUN FACTS ● FUN FACTS ● FUN FACTS

A mother hamster may have 13 babies at once!

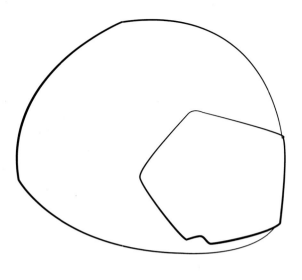

1. Here are the shapes for the head and body.

2. Draw in the face and the ears.

3. Add some little feet.

4. Color her body in brown.

Cat

This cat's body bends easily. This helps her to jump and climb.

She can see in the dark.

She wags her tail when she's angry.

She has sharp claws.

FUN FACTS ● FUN FACTS ● FUN FACTS ● FUN FACTS ● FUN FACTS

The pet cat is the smallest type of cat. The biggest is the tiger!

1. Most of this shape is her head.

2. Make her back bend like this.

3. Her tail is a bit like a question mark.

4. She's stripy like her cousin, the tiger.

Rabbit

His nose twitches when he smells food.

This rabbit has very long ears. He can hear well.

He has strong back legs for jumping.

He stamps with his feet if he's scared.

FUN FACTS ● FUN FACTS ● FUN FACTS ● FUN FACTS ● FUN FACTS

A father rabbit is called a buck. A mother rabbit is called a doe. A baby rabbit is called a kit!

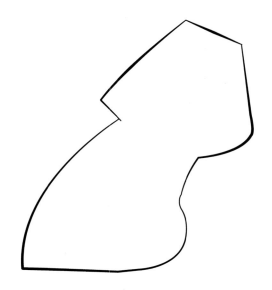

1. Start with this shape.

2. Ears make him look like a rabbit already!

3. He has really long front teeth.

4. Don't forget his fluffy tail.

Parakeet

This parakeet likes to eat seeds.

A parakeet is a type of small parrot.

Parakeets can be gray, blue, white, green, or yellow.

He has four toes on each foot.

FUN FACTS ● FUN FACTS ● FUN FACTS ● FUN FACTS ● FUN FACTS

Some parakeets can make noises that sound like people talking.

1. Here's a very easy shape.

2. Add the beak and the long tail feathers.

3. The wings are spread right out.

4. He is mostly green and yellow.

Horse

Horses can be many different colors. This one is brown and black.

Horses eat grass and hay.

Horses have long legs. They can run fast.

A horse's foot is called a hoof.

FUN FACTS ● FUN FACTS ● FUN FACTS ● FUN FACTS ● FUN FACTS

A horse can go to sleep standing up or lying down.

1. Draw this curvy shape.

2. Put in his face and two legs.

3. Make him stand on three legs.

4. Color him brown. Give him a long tail.

Pig

This pig has big, pointy ears.

His skin is covered with short hairs.

He digs for food with his nose.

He likes to roll in the mud to keep cool.

FUN FACTS ● FUN FACTS ● FUN FACTS ● FUN FACTS ● FUN FACTS

Some people keep pigs as pets!

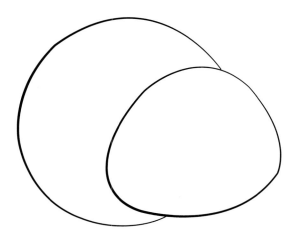

1. Draw two round shapes to start with.

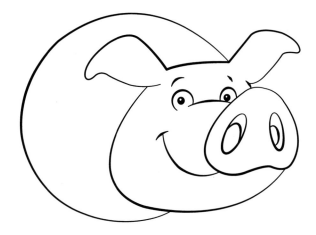

2. Add his ears, nose, and eyes.

3. Now draw his legs.

4. Don't forget his curly tail!

Cow

This cow has black and white spots.

She has small horns.

A cow's foot is called a hoof. It has two toes.

These are udders. Milk comes from here.

FUN FACTS ● FUN FACTS ● FUN FACTS ● FUN FACTS ● FUN FACTS

Cows curl their tongues around grass to pull it up.

1. Her body is shaped like the Moon.

2. Now add on the legs and the head.

3. She has a big mouth for eating lots of grass.

4. Underneath are her udders.

Sheep

This sheep has a woolly coat.

We use wool to make clothes.

Most sheep are white. They can also be black or brown.

She has short fur on her face and legs.

FUN FACTS ● FUN FACTS ● FUN FACTS ● FUN FACTS ● FUN FACTS

Sheep like to stay together. They always follow each other! A group of sheep is called a flock.

1. We start with a shape like a cloud.

2. Put the head at one end...

3. ...and some legs underneath.

4. She has a woolly tail.

Turtle

This turtle has a hard shell.

He can hide his head and legs inside his shell.

He digs a nest with his back legs.

Turtles eat grass, leaves, flowers, and fruit.

FUN FACTS ● FUN FACTS ● FUN FACTS ● FUN FACTS ● FUN FACTS

Turtles live for a very long time. Some turtles live more than 150 years!

1. Here's his shell. Everything's inside!

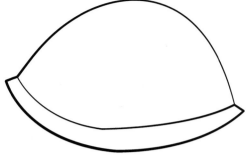

2. He's put his head and tail out.

3. And last come his legs.

4. His shell has a special pattern on it.

Chicken

The red part on top of her head is called a comb.

She has a pointy yellow beak.

She scrapes the ground with her feet. She looks for seeds and bugs to eat.

FUN FACTS ● FUN FACTS ● FUN FACTS ● FUN FACTS ● FUN FACTS

Chickens can fly. However they cannot fly very far.

1. Begin with this shape.

2. Her head goes at this end, her tail at the other.

3. Add a pair of strong scratchy feet.

4. She has a red comb on her head.

Duck

This duck eats plants, fish, and bugs.

She can use her wings to fly.

Ducks like to live near rivers and ponds.

She has webbed feet for swimming.

FUN FACTS ● FUN FACTS ● FUN FACTS ● FUN FACTS ● FUN FACTS

A duckling has a hard bump on its beak. This is called an egg tooth. It uses this to break out of its egg.

1. Draw this head, neck, and body.

2. She has a big beak.

3. She's not swimming. She's standing on the ground.

4. Draw her big, orange, webbed feet.

Donkey

This donkey has long pointy ears.

He has a thin, dark stripe along his back.

He is strong. He can carry heavy loads.

He can kick hard!

FUN FACTS ● FUN FACTS ● FUN FACTS ● FUN FACTS ● FUN FACTS

In some places, farmers keep donkeys with sheep. The donkeys scare wolves away from the sheep!

1. Draw his head and body shape.

2. He has very big ears.

3. Put three legs on the ground. The other leg is in the air.

4. He has a black tail and shiny hooves.

Glossary

comb something red on top of a chicken's head

curly shaped like a twist

fins a fish uses these to swim through the water

fluffy soft and furry

nest a place where an animal lays its eggs

pouch a space inside the cheek of an animal

tongue something inside your mouth that you use for speaking and eating

twitch move quickly up and down, or side to side

wag move from side to side

webbed feet feet with toes joined together by skin. Webbed feet help animals to swim.

whiskers long hairs on an animal's face. Animals use whiskers to feel things which are nearby.

wool soft, curly hair

woolly made from wool

Further Reading

Green, Dan. *How to Draw 101 Animals*. Top That! Kids, 2004.

Hayashi, Hikaru. *How to Draw Manga Volume 36: Animals*. Graphic-Sha, 2005.

Milbourne, Anna et al. *Drawing Animals*. E.D.C. Publishing, 2002.

Index